Olivia & Edmund
Ottawa Adventure!

By Christine Leger

Toby and Charlie were finally coming to visit! Olivia and Edmund raced around the house excitedly, fluffing pillows, dragging out sleeping bags, and sticking a big paper banner above the door: Welcome to Ottawa! It was late April, and the city was just waking up with spring—tiny green buds on trees, warm sunlight spilling through the windows, and the scent of earth returning to the air.

Olivia bounced on the balls of her feet, peering out the window. "They're here! They're here!" she squealed. Edmund, her older brother, scrambled to her side, his nose practically glued to the glass. A minivan pulled up to the curb, and out tumbled Toby and Charlie, their cousins from Toronto. Behind them emerged Ma Tante Sophie, Uncle Mark, Memere and Pepere!

The hugs and laughter were nonstop when Ma Tante Sophie, Uncle Mark, Memere, Pepere, and the cousins arrived. The driveway buzzed with suitcases, snacks, and overlapping stories. "We have so much to show you!" Edmund said, bouncing on his heels.

That night, the four kids set up a maze of pillows and blankets in one room, ready for the best sleepovers ever.

Their first stop was Parliament Hill. The grand stone buildings looked like castles, with tall towers and fluttering flags. They went down the stairs behind the Parliament and had a scenic view of the Ottawa River.

They walked along the Rideau Canal locks, where the water sparkled in the afternoon sun. Pepere told them stories of how the canal used to be a trade route, and in winter, it became the world's longest skating rink.

Next came the Bytown Museum, nestled beside the canal. Inside, creaky wooden floors and dusty displays told stories of how Ottawa grew from a lumber town into Canada's capital. Olivia loved the old log-driving tools. Edmund pretended to steer a raft down the river. "History is way cooler than I thought," said Toby.

Walked up the Sapier Bridge Memorial, to find the National War Memorial. The group fell quiet. Olivia watched Pepere remove his cap and bow his head. Toby squeezed Charlie's hand. "This place matters," she whispered.

THE FAMOUS FIVE

Not far away, five bronze women sat frozen in mid-conversation. "Who are they?" Charlie asked, staring at the confident faces and wide hats. "They're the Famous Five," Mom said. "They fought to make sure women were recognized as persons in Canada." Edmund blinked. "Wait... they weren't before?" Everyone nodded solemnly. It made the kids think a lot as they walked on.

They ran across the lawn, passing by Chateau Laurier and into nearby Major's Hill Park, where spring tulips were just beginning to peek from the soil. Then, towering over them like a giant space creature, stood the enormous spider statue they called Big Mama, just outside the National Gallery. "That's Big Maman," Olivia explained proudly. "She guards the art."

They crossed the Charlieandra Bridge high above the river, wind whipping their hair. Cars rumbled on one side, bikes zoomed past on the other. Olivia pointed out the view: water gleaming far below, the Parliament buildings standing tall behind them. The whole city stretched out in front of them like a treasure map, waiting to be explored.

The Canadian Museum of History was huge! While the adults explored ancient artifacts upstairs, the kids were set loose in the Children's Museum below. They climbed onto a pretend ship, made passports, wore clothes from around the world, and even helped "build" a house out of foam bricks. "Let's live here," Charlie declared, and nobody disagreed.

After all that walking, it was time for snacks! The Byward Market was bustling with street performers, fruit stalls, and the sweet smell of pastries. The kids each got a maple lollipop shaped like a leaf, which dripped deliciously down their fingers. Pepere treated himself to a bag of warm roasted almonds. "Best tour guides ever," he said, winking at Olivia.

At night, the house was filled with sleepy laughter. The four kids snuggled into one bedroom, whispering under the covers. They made up ghost stories, traded silly facts, and dared each other to stay up the latest. But one by one, they drifted off, surrounded by stuffed animals and the quiet comfort of being together.

The next day, they visited Hogs Back Falls where the water thundered over the rocks in white, frothy waves. Everyone got misted as they leaned over the rail to watch. "It sounds like a thousand drums!" Charlie shouted.

"See how the water splits right there?" he said. "That's the Rideau Canal! A long time ago, they built special locks to help boats go around the falls safely. It's like giving the boats their own secret staircase!"
He smiled and added, "They're officially called the Prince of Wales Falls—but everyone just calls them Hog's Back Falls. Sounds sillier, doesn't it?"

Then came the Diefenbunker—a real underground bunker from the Cold War! The air felt different underground, thick and quiet. The kids explored a command center, sat in a Prime Minister's emergency chair, and even saw the cafeteria frozen in time. "This is like a spy movie," whispered Toby.

They spent a sunny afternoon hiking at Mer Bleue Bog and Chapman Mills, where frogs croaked, birds sang, and boardwalk trails wound through marshes and woods. Grandma admired a curved wooden bridge and made everyone pose for a photo on it. "Nature and history," she said. "What a perfect pair."

It was the last thing they were doing today — and what a way to end it! They cheered until their voices cracked at the final women's hockey game of the season. The Ottawa Charge flew across the ice like rockets, chasing the puck incredibly fast. "I want to be that fast someday," said Edmund, eyes wide.

Olivia pumped her fists in the air as their team scored. Grandma wore a team scarf and clapped along happily.

"Let's take a day trip!" Uncle Mark exclaimed the next morning over breakfast. Everyone cheered. After consulting a map, they decided on a three-stop adventure: Watson's Mill, Omega Park, and the Five Span Bridge.

Their first stop was the Five Span Bridge in Pakenham, a unique stone bridge with five arches spanning the Mississippi River. They walked across the bridge, admiring the scenery and taking pictures.

Watson's Mill was their next stop, a beautifully preserved grist mill dating back to the 1800s. They learned about the process of grinding wheat into flour, and even got to try some freshly baked bread.

Their final stop was Omega Park, a wildlife park where they got to get up close with Canadian animals. They fed carrots to deer from their car windows, watched wolves howl, and saw bison grazing in the fields.

Finally, the day arrived when Toby and Charlie had to go home. There were hugs and promises to visit again soon. "Thank you for showing us Ottawa!" Toby said. "It was the best vacation ever!"

As the Honda Pilot pulled away, Olivia and Edmund waved goodbye, already looking forward to their next adventure with their cousins. Ottawa might be their hometown, but it was even more fun to explore with family.

"What should we do next time they visit Ottawa?"
Edmund asked her sister.

Olivia paused and smiled. "Maybe we'll take them to Parliament Hill for the Changing of the Guard Ceremony!"

Edmund considered this idea for a moment. "That sounds fun...or...maybe we will teach them to skate on the Rideau Canal in winter!"

Thinking of their next plans to explore Ottawa with Toby and Charlie, Olivia and Edmund walked back inside.